BLACK TRAILBLAZERS IN SPORTS

CHERYL MILLER

by David Lee Morgan Jr.

FOCUS READERS
NAVIGATOR

WWW.FOCUSREADERS.COM

Focus Readers is distributed by North Star Editions:
sales@northstareditions.com | 888-417-0195

Produced for Focus Readers by Red Line Editorial.

Photographs ©: Diane Johnson/Alamy, cover, 1; David Madison/Getty Images Sport/Getty Images, 4–5; G. F. Bryant/AP Images, 6; Jerry Wachter/Sports Illustrated/Getty Images, 8; Bob Riha Jr./Archive Photos/Getty Images, 10–11; Dennis Cook/AP Images, 13; Jim Rogash/Getty Images Sport/Getty Images, 15; Mike Powell/Getty Images Sport/Getty Images, 16–17; Wally McNamee/Corbis Historical/Getty Images, 19; Peter Read Miller/Sports Illustrated/Getty Images, 20; Allsport/Hulton Archive/Getty Images, 22–23; Bernstein Associates/Getty Images Sport/Getty Images, 25; Kirby Lee/AP Images, 27; Red Line Editorial, 29

Library of Congress Cataloging-in-Publication Data
Names: Morgan, David Lee, author.
Title: Cheryl Miller / by David Lee Morgan Jr.
Description: Mendota Heights, MN: Focus Readers, [2025] | Series: Black trailblazers in sports | Includes bibliographical references and index. | Audience: Grades 4-6
Identifiers: LCCN 2024000655 (print) | LCCN 2024000656 (ebook) | ISBN 9798889982098 (hardcover) | ISBN 9798889982654 (paperback) | ISBN 9798889983729 (pdf) | ISBN 9798889983217 (ebook)
Subjects: LCSH: Miller, Cheryl, 1964---Juvenile literature. | Women basketball players--United States--Biography--Juvenile literature. | African American women basketball players--Biography--Juvenile literature.
Classification: LCC GV884.M545 M67 2025 (print) | LCC GV884.M545 (ebook) | DDC 796.323092 [B]--dc23/eng/20240111
LC record available at https://lccn.loc.gov/2024000655
LC ebook record available at https://lccn.loc.gov/2024000656

Printed in the United States of America
Mankato, MN
082024

ABOUT THE AUTHOR

David Lee Morgan Jr. is the author of 11 books, including *LeBron James: The Rise of a Star* and *Breaking Through the Lines: The Marion Motley Story*. Morgan was a longtime sportswriter with the *Akron Beacon Journal* and is now a high school English teacher and public speaker.

TABLE OF CONTENTS

31

CHAPTER 1

HELLO, WORLD

In 1983, Cheryl Miller was in her first year at the University of Southern California (USC). But she was already a starter for the school's basketball team. That season, the USC Trojans reached the national championship game. They faced Louisiana Tech.

Going into the 1983 NCAA tournament, the University of Southern California had its best season ever. The team went 32–2.

Cheryl Miller (31) guards a Louisiana Tech player during the NCAA championship game.

Louisiana Tech had won the **inaugural** National Collegiate Athletic Association (NCAA) title the year before. Now, heading into the 1983 championship game, it was ranked No. 1 in the country. USC was ranked No. 2.

Miller played strong in the first half. She scored more than half of USC's points. Even so, USC trailed by 11 at halftime. Louisiana Tech seemed to be on its way to another championship.

However, Miller rallied her team in the second half. She played physically on offense. She made key baskets. And she drew foul after foul. Then she made most of her free throws.

Miller's intensity helped on defense, too. She grabbed rebounds and blocked shots. The Trojans slowly closed in on Louisiana Tech. They tied the game with about seven minutes to go. Then, with a few minutes left, they built a small lead.

Miller celebrates after winning the 1983 NCAA title.

The game came down to the final seconds. Louisiana Tech nearly tied it up. But the Trojans held on for a 69–67 win. It was their first national title in school history.

Miller had led the way with 27 points and nine rebounds. She was named the tournament's Most Outstanding Player.

The game was one of the first women's college basketball games on national TV. Millions of people watched. The game was a breakout event for women's basketball. As a result, the spotlight fell on Miller.

ALL-BLACK STARTING FIVE

USC made history when it won the 1983 NCAA title. The team was the first all-Black starting five to win a national championship. Miller played center. Twins Pam and Paula McGee played forward. Rhonda Windham started at point guard. And Cynthia Cooper played shooting guard.

CHAPTER 2

TALENTED FAMILY

Cheryl Miller was born on January 3, 1964, in Riverside, California. Cheryl had three brothers and a sister. They were an athletic family. All five kids played basketball. Her brother Darrell went on to play pro baseball. Her brother Reggie became a pro basketball star. Her sister, Tammy, excelled at volleyball.

Cheryl's family members were big supporters of her basketball dreams.

Cheryl started playing basketball at an early age. She used the hoop in her backyard. Cheryl practiced for hours. She joined teams whenever she could. But there weren't any girls' teams for her at first. So, she joined the boys' teams.

Cheryl's junior high had a girls' team. But some parents thought she played too physically. They tried to get her kicked off. This bothered Cheryl. She tried to join the boys' team. But the coach wouldn't let her. For a while, Cheryl felt as if she didn't belong anywhere.

That changed in high school. Cheryl joined the girls' team there. By then, she was already 6-foot-2 (188 cm). Because

Cheryl was named the country's high school athlete of the year in 1981 and 1982.

of her, the team became a powerhouse. Cheryl led her school to four straight state titles. The team won 132 games in those four years. It lost only four. At one point, the team won 84 games in a row.

Unlike other players, Cheryl focused on layups and offensive rebounds. So, she could take **high-percentage shots**. This turned her into a scoring machine. She even made history in her last year of high school. She scored 105 points in a single game. The length of games made her scoring even more impressive. They were

OUTDOING HER BROTHER

Two of Miller's 105 points came on a dunk. She was the first female player to dunk in an organized basketball game. Her brother Reggie also played in a game that day. He scored 40 points. At home, he bragged to Cheryl about it. He didn't know she had scored 105 points and had a dunk.

Reggie Miller (right) entered the Basketball Hall of Fame in 2012.

just 32 minutes long. In contrast, college and pro games last 40 minutes or more.

Cheryl earned national attention while still in high school. But that was just the start of her rise to the top.

USC
31

CHAPTER 3

COLLEGE SUPERSTAR

In 1982, Cheryl Miller was ready for the next level. Hundreds of colleges offered her **scholarships**. She picked USC. The school was close to her childhood home. Miller immediately became a star there.

The USC Trojans changed women's basketball. They brought Black basketball traditions to the women's game. For

In Miller's first year, USC head coach Linda Sharp said Miller was the best triple-threat player she'd ever seen.

example, the Trojans didn't wait to set up the offense before trying to score. Instead, USC's players quickly pushed the ball up the court. Then they went for the hoop within seconds.

Miller was the team's clear standout. And it wasn't just her scoring. She pulled down rebounds on both ends. She also got steals and made blocks. Miller was as big and strong as other centers. But she was faster than the guards. She never seemed to get tired, either.

As a result, the 1983 NCAA title was just the start. That summer, Miller earned a spot on Team USA. The team won gold in the Pan American Games in Venezuela.

Miller dribbles the ball during the gold medal game of the 1984 Olympics against South Korea.

The next year, she led the Trojans to their second straight NCAA title. Then she joined Team USA for the 1984 Olympics. Miller led her team to a gold medal there.

Miller (31) was the first basketball player, male or female, to have her jersey number retired at USC.

However, Miller's success didn't always turn into other opportunities. She believed it was because she was a Black woman. For example, a white gymnast named Mary Lou Retton also won gold in 1984. Retton got **endorsement** deals after. Miller had succeeded as much as Retton. But she did not get similar deals.

In 1985, *Sports Illustrated* named Miller the best college basketball player, male or female. She kept living up to it. In her time at USC, the team went 112–20. She scored 3,018 points. She was the second NCAA women's player with 3,000 points.

BEING BLACK AT USC

In the 1980s, USC students were mainly white and wealthy. Black athletes at USC faced racism at the school. They often felt as if they didn't belong. This was especially difficult for Miller's teammate Cynthia Cooper. She grew up very poor. As a result, Cooper faced sexism, racism, and classism.

CHAPTER 4

COACHING CAREER AND LEGACY

Cheryl Miller graduated from USC in 1986. She soon played in another **international** event. She was a member of Team USA in the Goodwill Games. This tournament took place in Moscow, Russia. Russia was then part of the **Soviet Union**.

The Soviet Union's team was the favorite. It had never lost an international

Miller celebrates after the 1986 Goodwill Games.

game at home. The team also featured Uljana Semjonova. She stood 7-foot-2 (218 cm). Many experts considered her to be the world's top female player.

But Miller and Team USA pulled off the **upset**. They beat the Soviet Union for the gold medal. The two teams had a rematch soon after. They faced off in the 1986 World Championships. Team USA won handily. Miller led the way.

However, Miller hurt her knee later that year. She never healed enough to play again. Even so, she remained a part of the game. She became a basketball **analyst** on TV. Miller also took up coaching. By 1995, her basketball **legacy** was clear.

Miller coached women's basketball at USC from 1993 to 1995.

She was voted into the Basketball Hall of Fame that year. Miller continued to break down barriers. In 1996, she became the first female analyst for a nationally televised NBA game.

The next year, a new pro women's basketball league formed. It was the

Women's National Basketball Association (WNBA). Some of Miller's former USC teammates joined as players. Miller stuck to coaching. She led the Phoenix Mercury to the Finals in 1998.

COACHING THE NEXT GREATS

Miller kept inspiring young players after her playing days were over. She became the women's basketball coach at USC in 1993. There, she coached Lisa Leslie and Tina Thompson. Leslie and Thompson became two of the first superstars of the WNBA. Leslie was the first player to dunk in a WNBA game. Thompson led the Houston Comets to four straight WNBA titles. In 2018, Thompson entered the Basketball Hall of Fame. Miller presented Thompson at the ceremony.

Miller was a reporter, analyst, and broadcaster for more than 15 years.

With her coaching, broadcasting, and mentoring of young players, Miller continued making an impact on women's basketball long after retiring.

CHERYL MILLER

- **Height:** 6 feet 3 inches (191 cm)
- **Weight:** 150 pounds (68 kg)
- **Born:** January 3, 1964
- **Birthplace:** Riverside, California
- **High school:** Riverside Polytechnic (Riverside, California)
- **College:** University of Southern California (Los Angeles, California) (1982–86)
- **Major achievements:** NCAA champion (1983–1984); Pan American Games gold medal (1983); Naismith Player of the Year (1984–86); Olympic gold medal (1984); Goodwill Games gold medal (1986); Naismith Memorial Basketball Hall of Fame (1995); Women's Basketball Hall of Fame (1999); International Basketball Hall of Fame (2010)

Los Angeles
Riverside
Phoenix
Moscow
Caracas

FOCUS ON CHERYL MILLER

Write your answers on a separate piece of paper.

1. Write a paragraph explaining the main ideas of Chapter 4.
2. In what ways do you think Cheryl Miller changed women's basketball?
3. What was the highest number of points Cheryl Miller scored in one game?

   A. 27
   B. 40
   C. 105

4. Why was Miller's basketball career cut short?

   A. She got cut from the team.
   B. She got injured.
   C. She wanted to focus on broadcasting.

Answer key on page 32.

GLOSSARY

analyst

A person who explains details about a certain topic.

endorsement

When athletes or celebrities get paid to use a company's product.

high-percentage shots

Shots that have a very good chance of going in.

inaugural

The first of a repeating event.

international

Having to do with many different countries.

legacy

The things a person becomes known for.

scholarships

Money given to students to pay for education expenses.

Soviet Union

A country in Europe and Asia that existed from 1922 to 1991.

upset

When a team wins a game that it was expected to lose.

TO LEARN MORE

BOOKS

Buckey, A. W. *Women in Basketball*. Mendota Heights, MN: Focus Readers, 2020.

Mahoney, Brian. *GOATs of Basketball*. Minneapolis: Abdo Publishing, 2022.

Solien, Paula. *12 Athletes Who Changed the World*. Mankato, MN: 12 Story Library, 2020.

NOTE TO EDUCATORS

Visit **www.focusreaders.com** to find lesson plans, activities, links, and other resources related to this title.

INDEX

Answer Key: 1. Answers will vary; **2.** Answers will vary; **3.** C; **4.** B